You can not lick your elbow!

And other things you should know…

Aaron Wayne-Duke

DEDICATION

Dara, Zion, Adam, Ayden and Jinx. My parents, John and Sherri Wayne and David and Janice Duke. The Wayne, Duke, Becker and Liniger families. Thank you.

Dream big, dream often. Then do everything you can to make those dreams come true.

Aaron

ACKNOWLEDGMENTS

Very special thanks to my illustrator Olivia Walker who brought my ideas to life with her wonderful art! Follow her on Instagram @oliviartist

Kevin and Kathy Clevenger thank you for your lifetime of love and support. To my high school journalism teacher, Sheryl Hinman, who encouraged me to continue writing. The parents and students at the Galesburg Academy of Martial Arts. To those that inspire me, John and Trina Pellegrini, John Graden, Brian Tracy, Soo Kon Kim, Jim Henson, John-Paul-George & Ringo, John Prine, Dr. Seuss, S.E. Hinton and the reason I wanted to become a radio DJ, Casey Kasem.

You can not lick
your elbow!

You'll look silly if you try!

You can not lick your elbow

Elephants can not jump. Chickens do not fly.

Snakes do not wear glasses!

Kangaroos do not play tambourine!

If you mix blue and yellow you will see the color green!

yellow

green

blue

Crocodiles can not stick out their tongue.

Cows do not wear shoes!

There have been
a dozen men
who walked
upon the moon!

Water is called H2O in basic chemistry!

Some people like wearing Hawaiian shirts just like me!

It is so much fun to learn and share with friends!

And now this book is finished because you are at the end!

ABOUT THE AUTHOR

Aaron Wayne-Duke was born and raised in Galesburg, Illinois. He is a former award winning radio broadcaster, voiceover artist, magazine columnist, public speaker and autism advocate. He has achieved black belts in the martial arts of Taekwondo and Hapkido. He continues to teach self-defense, personal protection and empowerment classes and seminars across the United States. "You can not lick your elbow" is his first book.

Follow Aaron on Twitter @AWaynesWorld or contact him through www.aaronwaynesworld.com.